MASTERING C++

A COMPREHENSIVE GUIDE TO PROGRAMMING EXCELLENCE

DR ASHOK JAHAGIRDAR PHD
(INFORMATION TECHNOLOGY)

Made with ♥ on the Notion Press Platform
www.notionpress.com

Contents

CHAPTER ONE

Introduction to C++

What is C++?

C++ is a powerful and versatile programming language that evolved from the original C language. Developed by Bjarne Stroustrup in the late 1970s at Bell Labs, C++ was designed with the goal of combining low-level efficiency with high-level abstractions. This makes C++ suitable for a wide range of applications, from system programming to game development and everything in between.

Origins and Evolution

To understand C++, it's essential to explore its roots in the C programming language. C, developed by Dennis Ritchie in the early 1970s, provided a procedural programming paradigm that became the foundation for many operating systems and software applications.

C++, introduced later by Stroustrup, built upon C by adding object-oriented programming features. The "++" in C++ reflects the language's evolutionary nature—incrementing from C. Over the years, C++ has undergone several standardizations, with the most recent versions (C++11, C++14, C++17, and C++20) introducing numerous features and improvements.

Why Learn C++?

C++ has stood the test of time and remains a crucial language in the software development landscape for several reasons:

Performance:

C++ provides low-level access to memory, allowing for efficient and fast code execution. This makes it a preferred choice for resource-intensive applications like game engines and operating systems.

Versatility:

C++ supports both procedural and object-oriented programming paradigms, giving developers the flexibility to choose the best approach for a particular task. This versatility makes C++ suitable for a wide range of applications.

Industry Usage:

C++ is heavily used in industries such as finance, gaming, embedded systems, and more. Many critical systems, including parts of major operating systems, are implemented in C++.

Object-Oriented Features:

C++ introduces powerful object-oriented programming features like classes and inheritance, enabling developers to create modular, reusable, and maintainable code.

Standard Template Library (STL):

The STL provides a rich collection of generic algorithms and data structures, streamlining development and reducing the need for reinventing the wheel.

As we delve deeper into this guide, you'll gain a comprehensive understanding of C++ and how to harness its capabilities to become a proficient programmer. Whether you're a novice or an experienced developer, mastering C++ opens the door to a world of programming possibilities.

CHAPTER TWO

Setting Up Your Development Environment

Installing a C++ Compiler

Before diving into C++ programming, you need a C++ compiler to translate your source code into machine code that a computer can execute. Several popular C++ compilers are available, and the choice often depends on your operating system:

For Windows:

You can use MinGW, Microsoft Visual C++, or Cygwin. MinGW is a popular choice for its simplicity and compatibility.

For macOS:

Xcode Command Line Tools include the Clang compiler. You can also use Homebrew to install GCC.

For Linux:

GCC (GNU Compiler Collection) is commonly used and can be installed using your distribution's package manager.

Ensure that your chosen compiler is properly installed and configured on your system. You can test this by opening a command prompt or terminal and typing the compiler's name (e.g., g++ for GCC). If the compiler is installed correctly, you should see information about its version and options.

Integrated Development Environments (IDEs)

While you can write C++ code using a simple text editor and compile it from the command line, using an Integrated Development Environment (IDE) can enhance your development experience. Some popular C++ IDEs include:

Visual Studio:

A powerful IDE for Windows with excellent C++ support. It includes a debugger, code editor, and project management features.

Code::Blocks:

An open-source, cross-platform IDE that supports multiple compilers. It's lightweight and suitable for beginners.

Eclipse:

A versatile IDE that supports various programming languages, including C++. It's platform-independent and extensible through plugins.

CLion:

A commercial IDE developed by JetBrains, known for its powerful code analysis and refactoring tools.

Choose an IDE that aligns with your preferences and operating system. The IDE simplifies tasks such as code navigation, debugging, and project management, providing a more efficient development workflow.

Configuring Your Workspace

Once you have your compiler and IDE set up, it's essential to configure your workspace for effective development:

Create a Project:

Most IDEs allow you to create projects to organize your code. A project typically includes source files, settings, and dependencies.

Configure Build Settings:

Set compiler options, linker settings, and other build configurations in your IDE. This ensures that your code compiles correctly and runs smoothly.

Version Control Integration:

If you're working on a larger project or collaborating with others, consider using version control systems like Git. Integrate version control into your IDE for easier collaboration and code management.

Explore IDE Features:

Familiarize yourself with features such as code autocompletion, syntax highlighting, and debugging tools. These features can significantly boost your productivity.

By the end of this chapter, you should have a fully functional C++ development environment. The right setup streamlines your coding process, allowing you to focus on writing quality code rather than dealing with configuration issues. In the next chapters, we'll start writing your first C++ programs and exploring the fundamentals of the language.

CHAPTER THREE

The Basics of C++

Understanding Syntax and Structure

C++ syntax builds upon the foundation of C, but with additional features. Here's a quick overview:

Comments:

Use // for **single-line comments** and
/* */ for **multi-line comments.**

```
// This is a single-line comment
/*
This is a
multi-line comment
*/
```

Statements and Blocks:

Statements end with a semicolon ;
Blocks are enclosed in curly braces {}

```
// Statement
int x = 5;
// Block
{
// Code inside the block
int y = 10;
}
```

Functions:

Functions are defined with a return type, name, parameters (if any), and a body.

```
// Function declaration
int add(int a, int b);
// Function definition
int add(int a, int b) {
return a + b;
}
```

Variables and Data Types

C++ supports various data types:

Integers:

int, long, short, etc.

```
int age = 25;
```

Floating-Point Numbers:

float, double

```
double pi = 3.14159;
```

Characters:

char

```
char grade = 'A';
```

Boolean:

bool

```
bool isStudent = true;
```

Strings:

```
#include <string>
std::string greeting = "Hello, World!";
```

Input and Output Operations:

Use cout for output and cin for input. Don't forget to include the <iostream> header.

```
#include <iostream>
int main() {
// Output
std::cout << "Hello, World!" << std::endl;
// Input
```

```
int num;
std::cout << "Enter a number: ";
std::cin >> num;
return 0;
}
```

Operators and Expressions:

C++ supports various operators:

Arithmetic Operators:

+, -, *, /, %

```
int result = 10 + 5; // result is 15
```

Relational Operators:

==, !=, <, >, <=, >=

```
bool isEqual = (x == y); // true if x is equal to y
```

Logical Operators:

&& (and), || (or), ! (not)

```
bool isTrue = (x > 0) && (y < 10); // true if x is positive and y is less than 10
```

Assignment Operator:

=

```
x = 20; // assign the value 20 to x
```

Increment/Decrement Operators:

++, --

```
int count = 5;
count++; // increment count by 1
```

Control Flow -Decision Making and Loops

if Statement:

```
int number = 15;
if (number > 10) {
std::cout << "Number is greater than 10." << std::endl;
} else {
std::cout << "Number is 10 or less." << std::endl;
}
```

switch Statement:

cpp

Copy code

```
int day = 3;
switch (day) {
case 1:
std::cout << "Monday" << std::endl;
break;
case 2:
std::cout << "Tuesday" << std::endl;
break;
// ... other cases ...
default:
std::cout << "Invalid day" << std::endl;
}
```

while Loop:

```
int i = 0;
while (i < 5) {
std::cout << i << std::endl;
i++;
}
```

for Loop:

```
for (int i = 0; i < 5; i++) {
std::cout << i << std::endl;
}
```

Understanding these basic concepts sets the foundation for more advanced C++ programming. In the upcoming chapters, we'll delve deeper into functions, object-oriented programming, memory management, and more.

C++ syntax builds upon the foundation of C, but with additional features. Here's a quick overview:

Comments:

Use // for single-line comments and /* */ for multi-line comments.

```
// This is a single-line comment
/*
This is a
multi-line comment
*/
```

Statements and Blocks: Statements end with a semicolon ;.

Blocks are enclosed in curly braces {}.

```
// Statement
int x = 5;
// Block
{
// Code inside the block
int y = 10;
}
```

Functions:

Functions are defined with a return type, name, parameters (if any), and a body.

```
// Function declaration
int add(int a, int b);
// Function definition
int add(int a, int b) {
return a + b;
}
```

CHAPTER FOUR

Functions and Modular Programming

Defining and Calling Functions

Functions in C++ play a crucial role in organizing code and promoting reusability. A function consists of a declaration, defining its purpose, and a call, invoking its execution.

Function Declaration:

```
// Function declaration
int add(int a, int b);
```

Function Definition:

```
// Function definition
int add(int a, int b) {
return a + b;
}
```

Function Call:

```
int result = add(5, 3); // result is 8
```

Function Parameters and Return Values

Parameters:

Functions can take parameters, which are values passed into the function. Parameters are specified in the function declaration and definition

```
// Function with parameters
```

```
void greet(std::string name) {
std::cout << "Hello, " << name << "!" << std::endl;
}
// Calling the function with a parameter
greet("Alice"); // Output: Hello, Alice!
```

Return Values:

Functions can return a value using the return statement. The return type is specified in the function declaration and definition.

```
// Function with a return value
int square(int num) {
return num * num;
}
// Calling the function and using the returned value
int result = square(4); // result is 16
```

Scope and Lifetime of Variables

Local variables:

Variables declared inside a function are local to that function, meaning they exist only within that function's scope.

```
void exampleFunction() {
int localVar = 10; // localVar is local to exampleFunction
std::cout << localVar << std::endl;
}
// Uncommenting the line below would result in a compilation error
// std::cout << localVar << std::endl;
```

Modular Programming Principles

Modular programming is an essential concept in C++. Breaking down a program into smaller, manageable modules (functions) enhances code readability and maintainability.

Header Files:

Declare functions in header files (.h) and define them in source files (.cpp). This separation allows for cleaner code organization.

```
// Example header file (example.h)
#ifndef EXAMPLE_H // Header guards to prevent multiple inclusions
#define EXAMPLE_H
#include <string>
// Function declaration
int add(int a, int b);
// Another function declaration
void greet(std::string name);
#endif
```

Source Files:

Define the functions in a source file (.cpp).

```
// Example source file (example.cpp)
#include "example.h" // Include the corresponding header file
// Function definition
int add(int a, int b) {
return a + b;
}
// Another function definition
void greet(std::string name) {
std::cout << "Hello, " << name << "!" << std::endl;
}
```

Main Program:

The main program includes the header files and uses the declared functions.

```
// Main program (main.cpp)
#include "example.h" // Include the header file
int main() {
int result = add(5, 3); // Using the add function
```

```
greet("Bob"); // Using the greet function
return 0;
}
```

Modular programming simplifies large codebases, promotes code reuse, and facilitates collaborative development. As you advance in your C++ journey, mastering these modular principles becomes increasingly valuable. In the next chapters, we'll explore object-oriented programming in C++, bringing even more structure to your code.

CHAPTER FIVE

Object-Oriented Programming (OOP) in C++

Introduction to Object-Oriented Concepts

Object-Oriented Programming (OOP) is a programming paradigm that uses objects—instances of classes—to organize and structure code. C++ supports the four main pillars of OOP:

Encapsulation:

Bundling data and functions that operate on that data into a single unit (class).

```
// Example of encapsulation
class Circle {
private:
double radius;
public:
void setRadius(double r) {
if (r > 0) {
radius = r;
}
}
```

```
double getArea() const {
return 3.14 * radius * radius;
}
};
```

Abstraction:

Hiding complex implementation details and exposing only what is necessary.

```
// Example of abstraction
class Car {
private:
int speed;
public:
void accelerate() {
speed += 10;
}
void brake() {
speed -= 10;
}
int getSpeed() const {
return speed;
}
};
```

Inheritance:

Creating a new class based on an existing class, inheriting its properties and behaviors.

```
// Example of inheritance
class Animal {
public:
void eat() {
std::cout << "Animal is eating." << std::endl;
}
};
class Dog : public Animal {
```

```
public:
void bark() {
std::cout << "Dog is barking." << std::endl;
}
};
```

Polymorphism:

Allowing objects of different types to be treated as objects of a common type.

```
// Example of polymorphism
class Shape {
public:
virtual void draw() const {
std::cout << "Drawing a shape." << std::endl;
}
};
class Circle : public Shape {
public:
void draw() const override {
std::cout << "Drawing a circle." << std::endl;
}
};
class Square : public Shape {
public:
void draw() const override {
std::cout << "Drawing a square." << std::endl;
}
};
```

Classes and Objects

A class is a blueprint for creating objects. An object is an instance of a class.

Defining a Class:

```
class Person {
private:
```

```
std::string name;
int age;
public:
// Constructor
Person(std::string n, int a) : name(n), age(a) {}
// Member functions
void displayInfo() const {
std::cout << "Name: " << name << ", Age: " << age <<
std::endl;
}
};
```

Creating Objects:

```
// Creating objects of the Person class
Person person1("Alice", 30);
Person person2("Bob", 25);
// Using member functions
person1.displayInfo(); // Output: Name: Alice, Age: 30
person2.displayInfo(); // Output: Name: Bob, Age: 25
```

Encapsulation and Abstraction

Encapsulation involves bundling data (attributes) and functions (methods) that operate on that data into a single unit—the class.

Abstraction is achieved by exposing only essential features of an object while hiding its internal complexities.

Encapsulation Example:

```
class BankAccount {
private:
std::string accountHolder;
double balance;
public:
BankAccount(std::string holder, double initialBalance) :
accountHolder(holder), balance(initialBalance) {}
void deposit(double amount) {
```

```
balance += amount;
}
void withdraw(double amount) {
if (amount <= balance) {
balance -= amount;
}
}
double getBalance() const {
return balance;
}
};
```

Abstraction Example:

```
BankAccount myAccount("Alice", 1000.0);
myAccount.deposit(500.0);
myAccount.withdraw(200.0);
std::cout << "Current Balance: $" << myAccount.getBalance() << std::endl;
```

Inheritance and Polymorphism

Inheritance allows a class to inherit properties and behaviors from another class. Polymorphism enables objects of different types to be treated as objects of a common type.

Inheritance Example:

cpp

Copy code

```
class Vehicle {
protected:
int speed;
public:
Vehicle(int s) : speed(s) {}
void displaySpeed() const {
std::cout << "Speed: " << speed << " km/h" << std::endl;
}
```

```
};
class Car : public Vehicle {
private:
std::string model;
public:
Car(int s, std::string m) : Vehicle(s), model(m) {}
void displayInfo() const {
std::cout << "Model: " << model << ", ";
displaySpeed();
}
};
```

Polymorphism Example:

cpp

Copy code

```
class Shape {
public:
virtual void draw() const {
std::cout << "Drawing a shape." << std::endl;
}
};
class Circle : public Shape {
public:
void draw() const override {
std::cout << "Drawing a circle." << std::endl;
}
};
class Square : public Shape {
public:
void draw() const override {
std::cout << "Drawing a square." << std::endl;
}
};
void drawShape(const Shape& shape) {
```

```
shape.draw();
}
```

Constructors and Destructors

Constructors initialize the object's attributes when an object is created. Destructors are called when an object goes out of scope.

Constructor Example:

cpp

Copy code

```
class Student {
private:
std::string name;
int age;
public:
// Parameterized constructor
Student(std::string n, int a) : name(n), age(a) {}
void displayInfo() const {
std::cout << "Name: " << name << ", Age: " << age << std::endl;
}
};
```

Destructor Example:

cpp

Copy code

```
class MyClass {
public:
// Constructor
MyClass() {
std::cout << "Constructor called." << std::endl;
}
// Destructor
~MyClass() {
std::cout << "Destructor called." << std::endl;
```

```
}
};
int main() {
MyClass obj; // Output: Constructor called
// The object goes out of scope, and the destructor is called
return 0; // Output: Destructor called
}
```

Understanding and applying object-oriented principles in C++ leads to more organized, flexible, and scalable code. In the upcoming chapters, we'll explore more advanced topics, including memory management and the Standard Template

CHAPTER SIX

Memory Management

Memory management in C++ involves dealing with pointers, references, and dynamic memory allocation.

Pointers:

A pointer is a variable that stores the memory address of another variable. It allows for direct manipulation of memory.

int number = 42;

int* pointerToNumber = &number; // pointerToNumber stores the address of number

// Accessing the value through the pointer

std::cout << "Value at address " << pointerToNumber << ": " << *pointerToNumber << std::endl;

References:

A reference is an alias for an existing variable. It provides an alternative way to access the same memory location.

int value = 100;

int& referenceToValue = value; // referenceToValue is a reference to value

// Modifying the value through the reference

referenceToValue = 200;

std::cout << "Value: " << value << std::endl; // Output: Value: 200

Dynamic Memory Allocation and Deallocation

Dynamic memory allocation allows you to allocate memory at runtime, giving you more flexibility.

Allocation with new:

int* dynamicNumber = new int; // Allocating memory for an integer

*dynamicNumber = 75; // Assigning a value to the dynamically allocated memory

// Deallocating memory with `delete`

delete dynamicNumber;

Array Allocation with new[]:

cpp

Copy code

int* dynamicArray = new int[5]; // Allocating memory for an array of integers

// Accessing elements of the dynamically allocated array

dynamicArray[0] = 10;

dynamicArray[1] = 20;

// Deallocating memory for the array

delete[] dynamicArray;

Memory Leaks and Best Practices

Memory leaks occur when allocated memory is not properly deallocated, leading to a loss of available memory over time.

Avoiding Memory Leaks:

// Correct usage of dynamic memory allocation and deallocation

int* dynamicValue = new int;

// ... use dynamicValue ...

delete dynamicValue; // Deallocate the memory when done

// Incorrect: Forgetting to deallocate memory

```
int* forgottenMemory = new int;
// ... use forgottenMemory ...
// Memory leak: No delete statement
// Incorrect: Deleting the same memory twice
int* doubleDelete = new int;
// ... use doubleDelete ...
delete doubleDelete;
// ... use doubleDelete ...
// Double delete: Results in undefined behavior
```

Smart Pointers:

Smart pointers, like std::unique_ptr and std::shared_ptr, manage memory automatically, reducing the risk of memory leaks.

```
#include <memory>
std::unique_ptr<int> smartNumber = std::make_unique<int>(42);
// No need to explicitly delete; memory is automatically managed by unique_ptr
std::shared_ptr<int> sharedNumber = std::make_shared<int>(100);
// Memory is automatically managed, and shared ownership is tracked
```

RAII (Resource Acquisition Is Initialization)

RAII is a C++ programming idiom where resource management (such as memory allocation) is tied to the lifespan of an object. Resources are acquired during the object's creation and released during its destruction.

RAII Example:

```
class FileHandler {
private:
FILE* file;
public:
FileHandler(const char* filename, const char* mode) {
```

```
file = fopen(filename, mode);
if (!file) {
throw std::runtime_error("Failed to open file.");
}
}
~FileHandler() {
if (file) {
fclose(file);
}
}
// Additional member functions for file operations
};
```

RAII ensures that the file is properly closed even if exceptions occur or the object goes out of scope.

Understanding and practicing good memory management techniques, such as using smart pointers and RAII, is crucial for writing robust and reliable C++ code. In the following chapters, we'll explore the Standard Template Library (STL) and more advanced C++ features.

CHAPTER SEVEN

Standard Template Library (STL)

The Standard Template Library (STL) is a powerful set of C++ template classes to provide general-purpose classes and functions. It includes various containers for storing and manipulating data efficiently.

Vector:

```
#include <vector>
// Declaration and initialization of a vector
std::vector<int> numbers = {1, 2, 3, 4, 5};
// Accessing elements
int firstElement = numbers[0]; // Accessing the first element
int lastElement = numbers.back(); // Accessing the last element
// Adding elements
numbers.push_back(6); // Adding 6 to the end of the vector
// Iterating through the vector
for (int num : numbers) {
std::cout << num << " ";
}
```

List:

cpp
Copy code

```
#include <list>
// Declaration and initialization of a list
std::list<std::string> names = {"Alice", "Bob", "Charlie"};
// Adding elements
names.push_front("David"); // Adding David to the front of the list
names.push_back("Eva"); // Adding Eva to the end of the list
// Removing elements
names.pop_front(); // Removing the first element
// Iterating through the list
for (const std::string& name : names) {
std::cout << name << " ";
}
```

Map:

```
#include <map>
// Declaration and initialization of a map
std::map<std::string, int> ageMap = {
{"Alice", 25},
{"Bob", 30},
{"Charlie", 22}
};
// Accessing elements
int bobAge = ageMap["Bob"]; // Accessing Bob's age
// Adding elements
ageMap["David"] = 28; // Adding David to the map with his age
// Iterating through the map
for (const auto& pair : ageMap) {
std::cout << pair.first << ": " << pair.second << " years old\n";
```

```
}
```

Algorithms: Sorting, Searching, and More

The STL provides a collection of algorithms that operate on containers, allowing you to perform various operations efficiently.

Sorting:

```
#include <algorithm>
// Sorting a vector
std::vector<int> numbers = {5, 2, 8, 1, 7};
std::sort(numbers.begin(), numbers.end()); // Sorting in ascending order
// Sorting a list
std::list<std::string> names = {"Bob", "Alice", "Charlie"};
names.sort(); // Sorting in lexicographical order
```

Searching:

cpp

Copy code

```
#include <algorithm>
// Searching for an element in a vector
std::vector<int> numbers = {1, 2, 3, 4, 5};
auto it = std::find(numbers.begin(), numbers.end(), 3); // Searching for the value 3
if (it != numbers.end()) {
std::cout << "Element found at position: " << std::distance(numbers.begin(), it) << std::endl;
} else {
std::cout << "Element not found." << std::endl;
}
```

Other Algorithms:

```
#include <algorithm>
// Other algorithms
std::vector<int> numbers = {1, 2, 3, 4, 5};
// Sum of elements
```

```
int sum = std::accumulate(numbers.begin(), numbers.end(), 0);
// Counting occurrences of a value
int countOfTwos = std::count(numbers.begin(), numbers.end(), 2);
// Transforming elements
std::vector<int> squaredNumbers;
std::transform(numbers.begin(), numbers.end(), std::back_inserter(squaredNumbers), [](int x) {
return x * x;
});
```

Iterators and Function Objects

Iterators provide a way to traverse the elements of a container, and function objects (functors) allow you to define custom operations to be applied to each element.

Iterators:

cpp

Copy code

```
#include <vector>
// Using iterators to traverse a vector
std::vector<int> numbers = {1, 2, 3, 4, 5};
// Using iterators in a for loop
for (auto it = numbers.begin(); it != numbers.end(); ++it) {
std::cout << *it << " ";
}
```

Function Objects (Functors):

```
#include <algorithm>
// Defining a functor
struct Square {
int operator()(int x) const {
return x * x;
}
```

```
};
// Using the functor with transform
std::vector<int> numbers = {1, 2, 3, 4, 5};
std::vector<int> squaredNumbers;
std::transform(numbers.begin(), numbers.end(), std::back_inserter(squaredNumbers), Square());
```

Using STL in Real-World Applications

The STL is a powerful tool for real-world applications, providing efficient and flexible data structures and algorithms. Here's a glimpse of using STL in a practical scenario.

Example: Word Frequency Counter

```
#include <iostream>
#include <fstream>
#include <sstream>
#include <map>
#include <vector>
#include <algorithm>
int main() {
// Read text from a file
std::ifstream file("sample.txt");
std::stringstream buffer;
buffer << file.rdbuf();
std::string text = buffer.str();
// Tokenize the text
std::istringstream iss(text);
std::vector<std::string> words(std::istream_iterator<std::string>{iss}, std::istream_iterator<std::string>());
// Count word frequencies
std::map<std::string, int> wordFrequency;
for (const auto& word : words) {
// Convert to lowercase for case-insensitive counting
```

```
std::string lowercaseWord = word;
std::transform(lowercaseWord.begin(),
lowercaseWord.end(), lowercaseWord.begin(), ::tolower);
// Increment the count
wordFrequency[lowercaseWord]++;
}
// Display word frequencies
for (const auto& pair : wordFrequency) {
std::cout << pair.first << ": " << pair.second << " times\
n";
}
return 0;
}
```

In this example, the STL components are used to read text from a file, tokenize it into words, and count the frequency of each word in a case-insensitive manner. This showcases the versatility and convenience of the STL in handling common tasks efficiently.

Understanding and mastering the STL is crucial for C++ developers, as it provides a rich set of tools for solving a wide range of programming challenges. In the upcoming chapters, we'll explore more advanced C++ features and techniques.

CHAPTER EIGHT

File Handling

Introduction to File I/O

File Input/Output (I/O) is a crucial aspect of programming, allowing you to read data from and write data to external files. C++ provides several classes and functions for file handling in the Standard Template Library (STL).

Reading from a File:

```
#include <iostream>
#include <fstream>
int main() {
// Open a file for reading
std::ifstream inputFile("example.txt");
// Check if the file is open
if (!inputFile.is_open()) {
std::cerr << "Error opening the file." << std::endl;
return 1; // Exit with an error code
}
// Read data from the file
std::string line;
while (std::getline(inputFile, line)) {
std::cout << line << std::endl;
}
// Close the file
```

```
inputFile.close();
return 0;
}
```

Writing to a File:

```
#include <iostream>
#include <fstream>
int main() {
// Open a file for writing
std::ofstream outputFile("output.txt");
// Check if the file is open
if (!outputFile.is_open()) {
std::cerr << "Error opening the file." << std::endl;
return 1; // Exit with an error code
}
// Write data to the file
outputFile << "Hello, File I/O!" << std::endl;
outputFile << "This is a new line." << std::endl;
// Close the file
outputFile.close();
return 0;
}
```

8.2 Binary File I/O

In addition to text file I/O, C++ also supports binary file I/O, allowing you to read and write binary data directly.

Reading Binary Data:

cpp

Copy code

```
#include <iostream>
#include <fstream>
struct Student {
int id;
std::string name;
double gpa;
```

```
};
int main() {
// Open a binary file for reading
std::ifstream binaryInputFile("students.bin",
std::ios::binary);
// Check if the file is open
if (!binaryInputFile.is_open()) {
std::cerr << "Error opening the binary file." << std::endl;
return 1; // Exit with an error code
}
// Read data from the binary file
Student student;
while
(binaryInputFile.read(reinterpret_cast<char*>(&student),
sizeof(Student))) {
std::cout << "ID: " << student.id << ", Name: " <<
student.name << ", GPA: " << student.gpa << std::endl;
}
// Close the binary file
binaryInputFile.close();
return 0;
}
```

Writing Binary Data:

cpp

Copy code

```
#include <iostream>
#include <fstream>
struct Student {
int id;
std::string name;
double gpa;
};
int main() {
```

```
// Open a binary file for writing
std::ofstream binaryOutputFile("students.bin", std::ios::binary);
// Check if the file is open
if (!binaryOutputFile.is_open()) {
std::cerr << "Error opening the binary file." << std::endl;
return 1; // Exit with an error code
}
// Write data to the binary file
Student student1 = {1, "Alice", 3.5};
Student student2 = {2, "Bob", 3.2};
binaryOutputFile.write(reinterpret_cast<const char*>(&student1), sizeof(Student));
binaryOutputFile.write(reinterpret_cast<const char*>(&student2), sizeof(Student));
// Close the binary file
binaryOutputFile.close();
return 0;
}
```

8.3 File Stream States and Error Handling

When working with file I/O, it's essential to check the state of the file streams and handle errors appropriately.

File Stream States:

cpp

Copy code

```
#include <iostream>
#include <fstream>
int main() {
// Open a file for reading
std::ifstream inputFile("example.txt");
// Check if the file is open
if (!inputFile.is_open()) {
std::cerr << "Error opening the file." << std::endl;
```

```
return 1; // Exit with an error code
}
// Check the stream state
if (inputFile.fail()) {
std::cerr << "Error reading from the file." << std::endl;
return 1; // Exit with an error code
}
// Read data from the file
std::string line;
while (std::getline(inputFile, line)) {
std::cout << line << std::endl;
}
// Check for errors after reading
if (inputFile.fail()) {
std::cerr << "Error reading from the file." << std::endl;
return 1; // Exit with an error code
}
// Close the file
inputFile.close();
return 0;
}
```

8.4 Random Access File I/O

C++ allows random access to files, enabling you to read or write data at any position within a file.

Random Access Reading:

cpp

Copy code

```
#include <iostream>
#include <fstream>
int main() {
// Open a file for random access reading
std::ifstream randomAccessFile("data.bin", std::ios::binary);
```

```
// Check if the file is open
if (!randomAccessFile.is_open()) {
std::cerr << "Error opening the file." << std::endl;
return 1; // Exit with an error code
}
// Set the read position to the 5th byte
randomAccessFile.seekg(4, std::ios::beg);
// Read an integer from the file
int value;
randomAccessFile.read(reinterpret_cast<char*>(&value), sizeof(int));
// Display the read value
std::cout << "Value at position 5: " << value << std::endl;
// Close the file
randomAccessFile.close();
return 0;
}
```

Random Access Writing

```
#include <iostream>
#include <fstream>
int main() {
// Open a file for random access writing
std::ofstream randomAccessFile("data.bin", std::ios::binary);
// Check if the file is open
if (!randomAccessFile.is_open()) {
std::cerr << "Error opening the file." << std::endl;
return 1; // Exit with an error code
}
// Set the write position to the 5th byte
randomAccessFile.seekp(4, std::ios::beg);
// Write an integer to the file
int value = 42;
```

```
randomAccessFile.write(reinterpret_cast<const char*>(&value), sizeof(int));
// Close the file
randomAccessFile.close();
return 0;
}
```

Understanding file handling in C++ is crucial for various applications, from simple text processing to complex data storage. In the next chapters, we'll explore more advanced topics in C++, including multi-threading and networking.

CHAPTER NINE

Exception Handling

Understanding Exceptions

Exception handling is a powerful mechanism in C++ for dealing with runtime errors. It allows you to detect and respond to exceptional conditions that may occur during program execution.

Basic Exception Handling:

```
#include <iostream>
int main() {
try {
// Code that might throw an exception
int divisor = 0;
int result = 10 / divisor;
// This code will not be executed if an exception occurs above
std::cout << "Result: " << result << std::endl;
} catch (const std::exception& e) {
// Catching and handling exceptions
std::cerr << "Exception caught: " << e.what() << std::endl;
}
return 0;
}
```

Throwing Exceptions

In C++, exceptions are thrown using the throw keyword. You can throw different types of exceptions, including built-in types and custom classes.

Throwing Built-in Types:

```
#include <iostream>
double divide(int numerator, int denominator) {
if (denominator == 0) {
throw std::runtime_error("Division by zero");
}
return static_cast<double>(numerator) / denominator;
}
int main() {
try {
double result = divide(10, 0);
std::cout << "Result: " << result << std::endl;
} catch (const std::exception& e) {
std::cerr << "Exception caught: " << e.what() << std::endl;
}
return 0;
}
```

Throwing Custom Exceptions:

```
#include <iostream>
#include <stdexcept>
class CustomException : public std::runtime_error {
public:
CustomException(const std::string& message) : std::runtime_error(message) {}
};
double divide(int numerator, int denominator) {
if (denominator == 0) {
throw CustomException("Custom Exception: Division by zero");
```

```
}
return static_cast<double>(numerator) / denominator;
}
int main() {
try {
double result = divide(10, 0);
std::cout << "Result: " << result << std::endl;
} catch (const std::exception& e) {
std::cerr << "Exception caught: " << e.what() <<
std::endl;
}
return 0;
}
```

Handling Multiple Exceptions

You can handle multiple types of exceptions by using multiple catch blocks.

```
#include <iostream>
#include <stdexcept>
void processInput(int value) {
if (value < 0) {
throw std::out_of_range("Input value is out of range");
} else if (value == 0) {
throw std::invalid_argument("Input value cannot be
zero");
} else {
// Process the input
std::cout << "Processing input: " << value << std::endl;
}
}
int main() {
try {
processInput(-5);
} catch (const std::out_of_range& e) {
```

```
std::cerr << "Out of Range Exception: " << e.what() <<
std::endl;
} catch (const std::invalid_argument& e) {
std::cerr << "Invalid Argument Exception: " << e.what()
<< std::endl;
} catch (const std::exception& e) {
// Catch any other exceptions
std::cerr << "Exception caught: " << e.what() <<
std::endl;
}
return 0;
}
```

The try, catch, throw, and finally Blocks

In C++, the try block is used to enclose the code that may throw exceptions. The catch block is used to catch and handle specific exceptions. The throw statement is used to throw an exception. However, C++ does not have a finally block like some other languages.

Using try, catch, and throw:

```
#include <iostream>
#include <stdexcept>
double divide(int numerator, int denominator) {
if (denominator == 0) {
throw std::runtime_error("Division by zero");
}
return static_cast<double>(numerator) / denominator;
}
int main() {
try {
double result = divide(10, 0);
std::cout << "Result: " << result << std::endl;
} catch (const std::exception& e) {
```

```
std::cerr << "Exception caught: " << e.what() << std::endl;
}
return 0;
}
```

RAII (Resource Acquisition Is Initialization) and Exception Safety

RAII is a key principle in C++ that promotes resource management through object lifetimes. It plays a crucial role in ensuring exception safety.

RAII Example:

```
#include <iostream>
#include <fstream>
#include <stdexcept>
class FileHandler {
private:
std::ofstream file;
public:
FileHandler(const std::string& filename) : file(filename) {
if (!file.is_open()) {
throw std::runtime_error("Failed to open file: " + filename);
}
std::cout << "File opened successfully." << std::endl;
}
~FileHandler() {
file.close();
std::cout << "File closed." << std::endl;
}
// Other member functions for file operations
};
int main() {
```

```
try {
FileHandler file("example.txt");
// Perform file operations
} catch (const std::exception& e) {
std::cerr << "Exception caught: " << e.what() <<
std::endl;
}
return 0;
}
```

Understanding and implementing exception handling is crucial for writing robust and reliable C++ programs. In the following chapters, we'll explore more advanced topics, including multi-threading and networking.

CHAPTER TEN

Best Practices and Coding Standards in C++

Importance of Coding Standards

Adhering to coding standards and best practices is essential for writing maintainable, readable, and efficient C++ code. It promotes consistency across projects and helps prevent common pitfalls.

Naming Conventions

Choosing meaningful and consistent names for variables, functions, classes, and other entities improves code readability.

Variable and Function Naming:

```
int calculateSum(int firstNumber, int secondNumber) {
// Function body
}
```

Class Naming:

```
class StudentRecord {
// Class members
};
```

Formatting and Indentation:

Consistent formatting and indentation enhance code readability. Choose a style and stick to it throughout your project.

Example:

```
#include <iostream>
int main() {
for (int i = 0; i < 10; ++i) {
if (i % 2 == 0) {
std::cout << "Even: " << i << std::endl;
} else {
std::cout << "Odd: " << i << std::endl;
}
}
return 0;
}
```

Coments and Documentation:

Effective use of comments and documentation helps others understand your code. Document complex algorithms, non-trivial functions, and important decisions.

Comments Example:

```
// This function calculates the factorial of a non-negative integer.
int calculateFactorial(int n) {
// Implementation details...
}
```

Avoiding Magic Numbers

Avoid using "magic numbers" (hard-coded numerical constants) in your code. Instead, use named constants or enumerations to improve code readability.

Magic Numbers Example:

```
// Avoid this
double calculateArea(double radius) {
return 3.14 * radius * radius;
```

```
}
// Prefer this
const double PI = 3.14;
double calculateArea(double radius) {
return PI * radius * radius;
}
```

Error Handling and Exceptions:

Handle errors gracefully using meaningful error messages and proper exception handling. Consider RAII principles for resource management.

Exception Handling Example:

```
try {
// Code that might throw exceptions
// ...
} catch (const std::exception& e) {
std::cerr << "Exception caught: " << e.what() << std::endl;
} catch (...) {
std::cerr << "Unknown exception caught." << std..endl;
}
```

Memory Management

Prefer smart pointers (such as std::unique_ptr and std::shared_ptr) over raw pointers to manage memory automatically and prevent memory leaks.

Smart Pointer Example:

```
#include <memory>
void exampleFunction() {
// Using std::unique_ptr
std::unique_ptr<int> uniquePtr = std::make_unique<int>(42);
// Using std::shared_ptr
std::shared_ptr<double> sharedPtr = std::make_shared<double>(3.14);
```

```
}
```

Const-Correctness:

Use const appropriately to make your code more robust and to indicate the intention of not modifying certain variables or objects.

Const-Correctness Example:

```
// Const-correct function
int calculateSum(const int& a, const int& b) {
// Parameters are not modified
return a + b;
}
// Const-correct class member function
class MyClass {
public:
int getValue() const {
// This function does not modify any member variables
return value;
}
private:
int value;
};
```

Avoiding Global Variables:

Minimize the use of global variables, as they can lead to various issues, including naming conflicts and difficulty in tracking changes.

Avoiding Global Variables:

```
// Avoid global variables
int globalVariable = 10;
int main() {
// ...
}
```

Unit Testing

Implement unit tests to ensure the correctness of your code. Utilize testing frameworks like Google Test or Catch to automate the testing process.

Unit Testing Example (Using Catch):

```
#define CATCH_CONFIG_MAIN
#include "catch.hpp"
int add(int a, int b) {
return a + b;
}
TEST_CASE("Adding two numbers", "[add]") {
REQUIRE(add(2, 3) == 5);
REQUIRE(add(-1, 1) == 0);
REQUIRE(add(0, 0) == 0);
}
```

Version Control:

Use version control systems (e.g., Git) to track changes, collaborate with others, and revert to previous states if needed.

Continuous Integration (CI):

Implement continuous integration practices to automate builds and run tests regularly. Popular CI tools include Jenkins, Travis CI, and GitHub Actions.

Keep Learning and Improving:

Stay updated with the latest C++ standards, practices, and tools. Embrace new features and techniques that can enhance your code.

Adhering to coding standards and best practices fosters a collaborative and efficient development environment. Consistency in style and approach across a codebase makes it easier for developers to understand, maintain, and extend the software.

Epilogue

As the author bids farewell to the readers, I express my gratitude to you for embarking on this intellectual voyage together. I also acknowledge the challenges you have overcome, the concepts you have mastered, and the skills you have honed.

I encourage you to continue pushing the boundaries of your programming prowess, and embrace a mindset of perpetual learning and innovation. One should note that true mastery is not an end but a beginning—it is only a catalyst for exploring new horizons in the dynamic world of C++.

I would like you to apply your newfound skills to real-world projects and challenges. One should remenber that the journey to programming excellence is an ongoing process—one that extends far beyond the confines of any book.

Together, let us , express our deep appreciation for the art and science of C++ programming.

This book is simply my commitment to excellence and the enduring pursuit of knowledge in the ever-evolving landscape of software development.

www.ingramcontent.com/pod-product-compliance
Lightning Source LLC
LaVergne TN
LVHW021202160826
845679LV00024B/2210

9798892771795